Money Struggles?

Don Barnes

Published by Don Barnes, 2024.

This publication provides the Author's opinion and neither the publisher nor the author intends to render legal, accounting, or other professional advice with this publication.
The publisher and the author disclaim any personal liability, loss or risk incurred as a consequence of the use and application, directly or indirectly, of advice, information or methods presented in this publication.
First Edition

Copyright © 2025

By Don Barnes / Tryune Works!

TRYUNE WORKS! and Life works in threes are trademarks and copyrights of Don Barnes and Tryune Works!

 **LifeWorksInThrees.com**

Table of Contents

About the Author

Don is the founder and author of Life Works in Threes!™ E-books. He is a lifelong Texan who has traveled extensively while taking a keen interest in human behavior. His curiosity about life and what drives humans led him to the discovery of how life works in threes. He coined this term as the *Tryune Concept.*

Don attended college on an athletic scholarship and then embarked on a 30-year career in the oil and gas industry. Since the year 2000, he has been a consultant for distributors and manufacturers of various industries. Along the way, he worked on his Tryune discovery in hopes of someday sharing his findings with those struggling unnecessarily... in life. What Don surmised from 40+ years of R&D was that people were struggling unnecessarily because they were not aware that "life works in threes." They, for the most part, have been living their lives <u>by chance</u> rather than <u>by choice,</u> he also discovered.

From this, he began focusing on the "mechanics of life" which shows formulas for success with subjects such as *life, health, money, purpose and so forth.* When people are able to grasp the Tryune Concept, they can apply the formulas with topics that interest them and begin eliminating the struggle. This epiphany is what triggered his Tryune venture and is now on the path of sharing with all who desire to improve on their lives.

Don currently resides in Southern California and Texas while overseeing his businesses and investments.

Life Works in Threes™

When I was a kid growing up, no one sat me down and said, "Okay Don, I'm going to show you how life works so that you can navigate your way through adulthood." I graduated from school, got married and went about my way with the "learn as you go" concept. It was kind of like putting together a backyard swing set without a set of instructions. Lots of frustration and do-overs, for sure!

My discovery of the "triune" word and noticing how things come together in threes is really what set me off on researching that maybe "life comes in three" …sort of a mechanical approach to managing life, if you will. I combed the libraries and bookstores for information on this and found one book on the subject that was written back in 1951. The author's name was John S. Arant.

What Mr. Arant had to say is this "For lack of a better name, I have called this *The Triangle of Triumph* and therefore, consistent with the name, since most of these conclusions are built on the geometric figure of the triangle." He continued "All Life and all lives are seated in, and circumscribed by, the triangle. The Author and Source and Director of all life is Himself triune in character – Father, Son, and Holy Spirit. Man is of triple nature – body, mind, and spirit – and within those three there are many triangles – desires, development, decay; intellect, will, sensibilities. Of this "paced interlude in the midst of eternity" which we call time there is the triangle of Past, Present, and Future. Space – that limitless and measureless element of the physical universe – is best known in terms of Height, Breadth, and Depth. Try building yourself some triangles along the lines of your Will, your Work, your Way – You will find some interesting angles.

So, for the first time, I realized that life is designed in a mechanical way to come in threes. That means you don't have to rely on wishing and hoping things turn out okay. You can actually look at the three parts that a particular thing is made of and then apply them to get what you're wanting. Like a three-ingredient recipe or a combination lock. With a combination lock, you need the three exact numbers to unlock the lock…otherwise you will continue to struggle.

Some 40 years later, I accumulated things that work in threes and that's when I knew I needed to share this with anyone wanting answers. To have success/harmony in your life, just apply the three parts of an area you're working on, and things will fall into place. I also learned that the recipe for success with just about anything is by doing these three things, consistently – THINK positively, SPEAK positively and ACT positively. For example, if I want to be a successful artist. I would think to myself "I can do this because I have the talent." Then I would speak it this way "Yes, I am working on my art degree and plan to do portraits professionally." Finally, I would act on that by taking art classes and continue crafting my skill. Eventually, I will see the positive results/success I'm looking for.

Conversely, if I think positively but speak negatively...it will cancel out. Or if I speak positively but have no positive action going on...nothing will happen.

I looked up "How Life Works" and "The Mechanics of Life" and these are really talking about the biology of how our cells work and other chemistry. TRYUNE WORKS! teaches that life is kind of like building blocks. Pick a topic you may be struggling with. See the three parts that topic consists of and then start applying them...on a consistent basis. That will help you overcome the struggle and get you back in harmony/success with how life works.

For 30+ years I was a golf instructor (by accident). My two kids had some success playing junior golf and so friends and neighbors would ask me to show them and their kids how to play golf successfully. From all of this, I got pretty good at watching golfers on the driving range and could spot right away why they were struggling with hitting bad golf shots. I was able to do that because I knew the three steps to hitting good golf shots. I learned them from studying golf and played for several decades. I "broke the code" for me so to speak.

So now you know that life works in threes. You can live your life *by choice* rather than *by chance* and that my friend... is the key to a fulfilling life.

LIFE WORKS
IN THREES!

My sanctuary on the Pacific coast

Introduction

Financial literacy is not merely a skill set; it's a fundamental aspect of survival in today's complex world. Without it, individuals are vulnerable to making poor financial decisions that can have long-lasting consequences. Being financially literate means understanding how money works, from budgeting and saving to investing and managing debt. These skills empower individuals to navigate economic uncertainties, unexpected expenses, and retirement planning with confidence and foresight.

In a practical sense, financial literacy equips individuals to make informed choices about their spending habits and savings goals. It enables them to distinguish between needs and wants, prioritize financial goals, and develop strategies to achieve them. Without this knowledge, people may fall prey to predatory financial practices, accumulate unsustainable debt, or fail to build a secure financial future for themselves and their families.

Moreover, financial literacy extends beyond personal finance; it fosters economic stability and growth at both individual and societal levels. When people are financially literate, they are more likely to contribute positively to the economy through responsible borrowing, prudent investing, and entrepreneurial ventures. This contributes to overall economic resilience and reduces the burden on social welfare systems, thereby benefiting society as a whole.

In essence, being financially literate is not just about balancing a checkbook or understanding interest rates; it's about survival in an increasingly interconnected and competitive world. It empowers individuals to weather financial storms, seize opportunities, and build a secure foundation for themselves and future generations. Therefore, promoting and enhancing financial literacy should be a priority in education and public policy to ensure that everyone has the knowledge and skills necessary to thrive in today's economic landscape.

My discovery of the Tryune Concept

Before we dive into money struggles and how to overcome them, let me share my discovery of the Tryune Concept and how life works in threes. It all began in the summer of 1982.

I grew up with parents who treated everyone with decency and respect. My three older sisters and I were raised in a home that was "middle-class traditional." We lived in modest homes in different small towns, attended school and church on a regular basis and celebrated all the traditional holidays. Eventually we settled during the spring of 1964 in the big city of Houston, Texas. I'll never forget the vastness of the city and hearing sirens from police cars, fire trucks and ambulances on a regular basis. I was excited and scared at the same time.

Once settled in this fast-paced city, I finished my growing-up years with an academic diploma and sweetheart intact. I got a job, bought a car, got married, bought a house and produced two beautiful babies in a span of about 5 years. Talk about having to grow up fast!

Things went from great in my childhood to absolute misery in my young adulthood. I began to struggle with my job because deep down I just hated what I was doing. This problem created a snowball effect because soon after, my weight, my finances, my relationships, my happiness and everything else worth saving was going down the drain. I eventually hit a level of frustration that I had never experienced before and didn't know how to get out of it. My cry for help was for anyone or anything to come to my rescue. I just ran out of solutions for my situation.

This is when my discovery happened.

One night shortly after my meltdown, while sleeping soundly, the word "triune" began to softly pound in my head like a mantra. I woke up a little startled and decided to go look up the word in my favorite dictionary (this was WAY before Google.) The definition said '**triune** (try-une) – 1) a group of three things; united. 2) Being 3 in 1 such as *humans are mental, physical and spiritual.* I scratched my head, got a glass of water and went back to bed.

The next day while driving around town, I began thinking about things that I was taught in my younger years that came in threes. My Boy Scout manual taught that to have **character**, I needed to be *1) physically strong,* 2) *mentally awake* and 3) *morally straight.* My high school football coach would say emphatically "If you want to be **a good football player**, you have to be *1) mobile 2) agile* and *3) hostile*!" My first sales manager shared with me that to be **a successful salesman**, I needed to have *1) sales skills, 2) product knowledge and 3) a good image.*

"Hmm", I thought, "wonder if there are other examples out there of things that work in threes?" So, some 40 years later, I have researched and discovered that many, many things work in threes. What this message was telling me is that to achieve success or balance in any significant area of my life, the three things that area consisted of had to be present continuously. That's when I had my epiphany. This discovery was telling me the secret to how life <u>really</u> works.

Tryune is a play on the word "triune" as an invitation to "try" this concept. Furthermore, we do not say that life <u>only</u> works in threes. Life also works in ones, twos, fours and so on. What has been observed though is that the many things significant to life, just so happen to come and work in threes. That's what is being shared in this book.

Now, you are about to see 40+ years of research and proof that life works in threes. I did not make up any of these topics. I invite you to research them on the internet to validate what is written here. There are some interesting facts that most of us have never realized...until now.

How Life Works in Threes (around 200 examples)

<u>LIFE</u>

Humans consist of *body, mind and soul.*

A human's basic needs are *health, income and provisions.*

A human's basic wants are *comfort, gain and approval.*

Our minds are made up of the *conscious, the subconscious and the unconscious.*

Philosophy explains *the id, the ego and superego.*

Atoms consist of *protons, neutrons and electrons.*

Motion is explained by *three basic laws.*

Science falls under three main branches: *natural, social and formal sciences*

Time is *past, present and future...*at the same time.

Electricity consists of *ohms, amperes and voltage.*

Music's basic elements are *duration, pitch and timbre.*

Democracy is a government *of the people, by the people and for the people.*

U.S. branches of government are *the judicial, the executive and the legislative.*

Armed Forces protect us on *land, air and sea.*

Environmentally, we are asked *to reduce, recycle and re-use.*

The news program gives us *the news, sports and conditions.*

Our days consist of *morning, afternoon and evening.*

Three months in each season of the year

Our main meals are known as *breakfast, lunch and dinner.*

A balanced diet consists of *good proteins, carbohydrates and fats.*

Traditional Family consists of *father, mother, and child(ren)*

<u>SCIENCES</u>

Three major branches of natural science – *(physical, earth/space and life sciences)*

Three major branches of modern physics - *(classical, relativistic, quantum)*

Three major branches of biology *(botany, zoology, microbiology)*

Three spatial dimensions: *height* (up/down), *width* (left/right) and *depth* (forwards/backwards)

Three-gauge bosons (photon, gluon, W&Z bosons)

Three types of elementary particles *(leptons, quarks, gauge bosons)*

Three quarks in every proton *(two "up" and one "down")*

Three primary colors of light *(red, green, blue)*

Three color tone properties *(hue, value, chroma)*

Three laws of motion (*Newton's laws*)

Three laws of planetary motion (*Kepler's laws*)

Three layers of the Sun's interior (*core, radiative zone, convective zone*)

Three layers of the Sun's atmosphere (*photosphere, chromosphere, corona*)

Three types of meteorites (*iron, stony iron, stony*)

Three types of galaxy shapes (*elliptical, spiral, irregular*)

Three substances of the universe (*normal matter, 'dark matter', 'dark energy'*)

Three phases of the moon (*new moon, first quarter, full moon*)

Three planetary regions (*temperate, sub-tropical, tropical*)

Three layers of the Earth (*crust, mantle, core*)

Three components of an ecosystem (*producers, consumers, decomposers*)

Three types of rocks (*igneous, sedimentary, metamorphic*)

Three types of fossil fuels (*coal, crude oil, natural gas*)

Three hydrological processes (*evaporation, condensation, precipitation*)

Three basic types of (meteorological) precipitation (*liquid, freezing, frozen*)

Three types of substances (*mono-constituent, multi-constituent, UVCB*)

Three phases of (normal) matter (*solid, liquid, gas*)

Three types of covalent chemical bonds (*single, double and triple bonds*)

Three isotopes of hydrogen (*protium, deuterium, tritium*)

Three atoms in each molecule of water (*two hydrogen atoms and an oxygen atom*)

Three endings to salts *(-ide, -ite, -ate)*

Three requirements for fire *(fuel, oxygen, heat)*

Three nucleotide bases in a genetic codon

Three domains of life *(archaea, bacteria and eukaryotes)*

Three major groups of flowering plants *(monocots, eudicots, magnolids)*

Three major functions that are basic to plant growth and development: *(photosynthesis* [making sugars], *respiration* [metabolizing those sugars], and *transpiration* [water vapor loss]

Three things that the chlorophyll in plants needs for photosynthesis to take place: *(sunlight, carbon dioxide and water)*

Transpiration serves three roles: *(cooling the plant, moving minerals* and *sugars through the plant,* and *maintaining the turgidity pressure* [stiffness] *of the plant's cells)*

Three parts of an insect's body *(head, thorax, abdomen)*

BIOLOGY

Three types of cones in the retina, relating to the three primary colors

Three semi-circular canals in the ear *(lateral, anterior, posterior)*

Three sections in the ear *(outer, middle, inner)*

Three ossicles in the middle ear *(malleus, incus, stapes)*

Three segments to each limb *(proximal, mid, distal)*

Three bones in each arm *(humerus, radius, ulna)*

Three joints in the arm *(shoulder, elbow, wrist)*

Three joints in the leg *(hip, knee, ankle)*

Three joints in the elbow *(humeroulnar, humeroradial, proximal radioulnar)*

Three functional compartments in the knee joint (*the femoropatellar, medial femorotibial* and *lateral femorotibial articulations*)

Three types of fibrous joints (*sutures, gomphoses, syndesmoses*)

Three types of bone in each hand (*carpals, metacarpals, phalanges*)

Three types of bone in each foot (*tarsals, metatarsals, phalanges*)

Three bones (phalanges) in each finger and in each toe (*proximal, intermediate, distal*)

Three layers of skin (*dermis, epidermis, hypodermis*)

Three components of a cell (*cell membrane, nucleus, cytoplasm*)

Three types of blood vessels (*arteries, veins, capillaries*)

Three types of blood cells [*red* (erythrocytes), *white* (leukocytes), *platelets* (thrombocytes)]

Three processes of the intestinal tract (*ingestion, digestion, excretion*)

Three germ layers (*Endoderm, Mesoderm, Ectoderm*)

Three parts of a human tooth (*crown, neck, root*)

Three organs of otolaryngology (*ear, nose, throat*)

Three major body systems (*digestive, circulatory, respiratory*)

Three parts to a neuron: (*soma* [*cell body*], *axon, dendrites*)

Three main parts of the brain (*forebrain, midbrain, hindbrain*)

Three parts of the forebrain (*cerebrum, thalamus, hypothalamus*)

Three parts of the midbrain (*colliculi, tegmentum, cerebral peduncles*)

Three parts of the hindbrain (*cerebellum, pons, medulla*)

Three membranes enclosing the brain (*dura mater, arachnoid, pia mater*)

The brain operates on three levels: *consciously* (for cognitive thought and declarative memory); *subconsciously* (for pre-planned actions and procedural memory); and *unconsciously* (for breathing, heart beating, etc.)

Our conscious mind is fed from three sources: *our senses* (which can be fooled); *our memory* (which is flawed); and *our imagination* (which is inventive)

Three aspects of the human mind (*memory, intellect, will*)

Three parts of the human personality (*id, ego, superego*)

The sum of human capacity consists of three abilities (*thought, word and deed*)

Three times of man (*birth, life, death*)

Three periods of the Gait Cycle (*initial double limb support, single limb support, and terminal double limb support*)

MUSIC

Three types of musical notes (*sharps, flats, naturals*)

Three aspects of a song (*lyrics, melody, rhythm*)

Three types of musical chords (*root, third, fifth*)

MATHEMATICS

Three types of a real number (*positive, negative, zero*)

Three parts to any arithmetic operation: for addition: *augend, addend and sum* - for subtraction: *minuend, subtrahend and difference* - for multiplication: *multiplicand, multiplier and product* - for division: *dividend, divisor and quotient*

Three laws of arithmetic operations (*commutative, associative, distributive*)

Three types of equivalence relation (*reflexivity, symmetry, transitivity*)

Three types of symmetry operations (*translation, rotation, reflection*)

Three geometries (*Euclidean, spherical, hyperbolic*)

The number *3* is the basis of an entire branch of mathematics, called trigonometry (from the Greek *trigonon* "triangle" + *metron* "measure")

Three trigonometric functions (*sine, cosine, tangent*)

Three types of average (*mean, mode, median*)

GRAMMAR

Three logical operators (*AND, OR and NOT*)

Three laws of logic (*identity, noncontradiction, excluded middle*)

Three parts of a logical syllogism (*major premise, minor premise, conclusion*)

Three grammatical parts to a sentence (*subject, verb, complement*)

Three persons in grammar [*1st person* (I/we), *2nd* (you or your), *3rd* (he/she/it/they)]

Three genders in grammar [*masculine* (he/him), *feminine* (she/her), *neuter* (it)]

Three forms of comparison in grammar [*positive, comparative* (more, -er), *superlative* (most, -est)]

Three cases in (English) grammar [*subjective/nominative* (he), *objective/accusative* (him) and *possessive/genitive* (his)]

Three parts of a narrative (*beginning, middle, end*)

Components of an essay (*introduction, body, conclusion*)

Elements of a rhetorical appeal (*ethos, pathos, logos*)

Aspects of a story (*plot, characters, setting*)

RELIGION

The Creator – *omniscient, omnipotent, omnipresent*

Christian God – *Father, Son, Holy Spirit*

Jesus – *The Way, The Truth, The Life*

Ancient Near East- *Qudshu, Astarte, Anat*

Classical Antiquity – Many dieties came in threes

Hinduism – Para Brahman is *Brahma, Visnu, Shiva*

Ancient Celtic Cultures – *many example of triad dieties*

Buddhism – *The three jewels*

Taoism – *The three pure ones*

Islam – *Fear, Hope and Love*

Baha'i - *Intention, Power and Action*

Confucianism – *Benevolence, Wisdom and Courage*

<u>OTHER TRIUNE EXAMPLES</u>

3 Coins in a Fountain

3 Days of the Condor

3 Miles in a League

3 Goals in a Hat Trick

3 Piece Suit

3 Feet in a Yard

3 Books in Lord of the Rings

3 Ring Circus

3 Ships of Christopher Columbus

3 Sheets to the Wind

3 Books in a Trilogy

3 Wheels on a Tricycle

3 Wise Men

3-Legged Race

3 Ring Circus

3-Wheeler

3 Cornered Hat

3 Dimensional

3 Musketeers

3 R's (reading, 'riting, 'rithmatic)

3 Sides of a triangle

3 Races in the Triple Crown (horse racing)

3 Angles in a Triangle

3 Trimesters in a Pregnancy

3 Flavors in Neapolitan Ice Cream

3 Stars in Orion's belt

3 Barleycorns in an Inch

3 Hands on a Clock (with the Seconds Hand)

3 Colors in a Flag

3 Minute Egg

3 Great Pyramids at Giza

3 Holes in a Bowling Ball

3 Colors in a Set of Traffic Lights

3 Minutes in a Boxing Round

3 Teaspoons in a Tablespoon

3 Legs on a Stool

3 Monastic Vows (Obience, Stability, Conversatio Morum)

3 Body Types: Endomorph, Mesomorph, Ectomorph

3 Ring Notebooks

3 Germ layers: Endoderm, Mesoderm, Ectoderm

3 Species of Homo: Homo habilis, Homo erectus, Homo sapiens

3 Basic parts of a camera: Lens, Shutter, Sensor

3 Stages of a Project lifecycle: initiation, planning, execution

The Truth, The Whole Truth and Nothing but the Truth

Life, Liberty and the Pursuit of Happiness

Hear no Evil, See no Evil, Speak no Evil

National motto of France/Haiti: Liberty, Equality, Fraternity

Paper, Rock, Scissors

Ready, Aim, Fire

On Your mark, Get Set, Go

Olympic medals of gold, silver, bronze

Types of joints (ball & socket, hinge, pivot)

Stages of a rocket launch (launch, orbit, re-entry)

Parts of a joke (setup, delivery, punchline)

Primary components of a transistor (emitter, base, collector)

Primary components of an airplane (fuselage, wings, empennage)

Basic components of a computer: CPU, memory, storage

Three phases in the development of technology (*eotechnic* [*mechanical*], *paleotechnic* [*steam-powered*] and *neotechnic* [*electric-powered*]

Communication systems require three components (*transmitter, channel, receiver*)

The list goes on. See if you can find more examples as they are everywhere in our universe! Now that you know that life works in threes (with proof!), we can begin to apply this concept to whatever topics we want.

So, to overcome struggles with money, we need to apply the three areas that money consists of – FLOW, SAVE and SPEND. Let's get started!

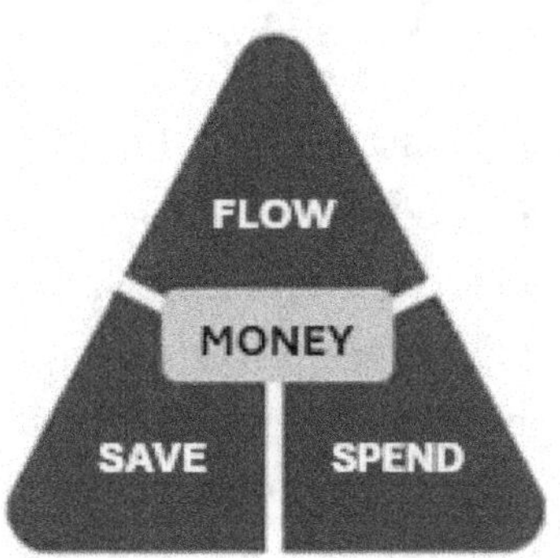

FLOW
MONEY
SAVE
SPEND

MONEY

Let's take a fun trip back in time to when the idea of money first popped up in human history. Picture this: way back in ancient times, people started trading goods with each other. Maybe someone had an extra bushel of grain, and another person had a shiny rock they didn't need. They figured out that by swapping these items, they could both get something they wanted. Pretty cool, right?

As communities grew and trading became more common, people started to realize that some items were easier to trade than others. Imagine trying to carry around a herd of sheep just to buy a loaf of bread – not very practical! So, clever folks came up with the idea of using something that everyone agreed had value, like shiny metals or rare shells. These became the first forms of money – objects that represented worth and made trading a whole lot easier.

Fast forward a bit, civilizations around the world began to create coins made from metals like gold and silver. These were stamped with symbols to show their value and became a universal way to buy and sell goods. Eventually, paper money came into play, making transactions even simpler. Today, we've got digital money flying around the internet! It's amazing how an idea born out of simple trading has evolved into the complex financial systems we use today. So, next time you pull out your wallet or tap your phone to pay, remember you're part of a long, fascinating history of human ingenuity and creativity in making life a little more convenient for everyone!

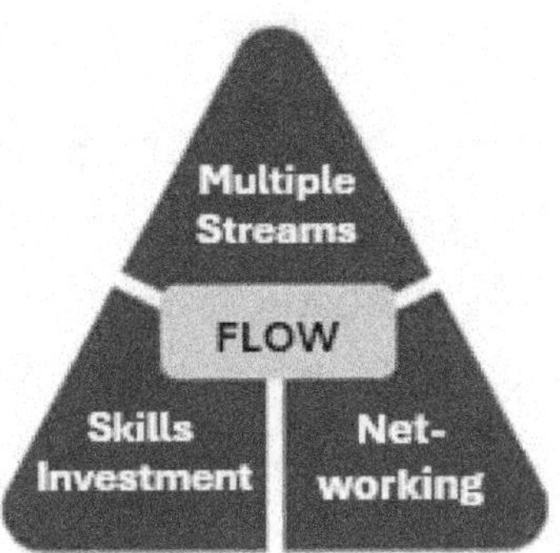
Multiple
Streams
FLOW
Skills
Investment
Net-
working

FLOW

When it comes to earning money, there's a wide world of work out there waiting for us to explore. Let's start with traditional jobs. These are the ones you might find in offices, shops, or factories – like being a teacher, a nurse, a chef, or even a software engineer. These jobs often involve working for a company or organization, where you exchange your time and skills for a paycheck. They provide stability and a regular income, which can be reassuring when planning for the future.

Then there's freelance and gig work. This type of work is all about flexibility and independence. Freelancers are their own bosses, offering services like graphic design, writing, tutoring, or driving for ride-sharing apps. Gig work often involves short-term projects or tasks, like delivering groceries or renting out a spare room through platforms like Airbnb. It's a great way to earn money on your own schedule and explore different interests and skills.

And let's not forget about entrepreneurship! Starting your own business is like planting a seed and watching it grow into something amazing. Whether it's opening a bakery, launching a tech startup, or selling handmade crafts online, entrepreneurship is all about taking risks, being creative, and turning your passion into profit. It can be challenging, but also incredibly rewarding, as you have the freedom to shape your own destiny and create something that brings value to others.

So whether you're drawn to a traditional job with stability, the freedom of freelance work, or the excitement of entrepreneurship, there's a world of opportunities out there to earn money doing what you love. Finding the right path for you might take some exploration and experimentation, but with determination and a positive attitude, you can carve out a fulfilling career that not only pays the bills but also brings you joy and fulfillment. Here's to finding your passion and turning it into a paycheck!

Creating flows of money requires a combination of strategic planning, proactive effort, and a mindset geared towards growth and opportunity. Here are three keys to effectively generating income streams:

1. **Diversification and Multiple Income Sources**: Relying on a single source of income can be risky. Diversifying your income streams spreads out risk and increases your overall financial stability. This can include having a primary job or business while also exploring side hustles, investments, rental income, or freelancing opportunities. Each additional income stream not only provides financial support but also enhances your resilience against economic downturns or job instability.

2. **Investing in Skills and Education**: Continuous learning and skill development are essential for staying competitive in the marketplace. Investing in education, whether formal (like degrees or certifications) or informal (like online courses and workshops), enhances your value proposition to employers or clients. It also opens up new opportunities for career advancement, higher-paying jobs, or starting your own business. By constantly upgrading your skills, you increase your earning potential and maintain relevance in a rapidly changing economy.

3. **Building and Leveraging Networks**: Networking is crucial for creating opportunities for income generation. Building strong professional relationships can lead to job referrals, business partnerships, mentorship, and access to valuable resources. Networking platforms, industry events, and social media can all be utilized to expand your network. Additionally, maintaining a positive reputation and delivering quality work or services are key to fostering long-term relationships that can sustain and grow your income streams over time.

By implementing these keys—diversifying income sources, investing in skills, and leveraging networks—you can establish and maintain multiple flows of money coming your way. This not only provides financial security but also positions you to capitalize on emerging opportunities and achieve long-term financial goals.

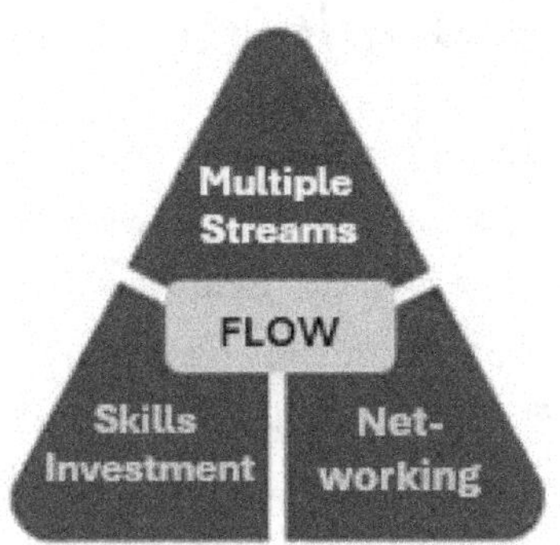
Multiple
Streams
FLOW
Skills
Investment
Net-
working

Multiple Streams

Creating multiple streams of income is a strategic approach to bolstering financial stability and enhancing overall wealth. Diversifying income sources reduces dependence on a single paycheck or business venture, thereby spreading risk and increasing resilience against economic fluctuations. One effective method is to start small, perhaps with a side hustle or freelance work that aligns with your skills or interests. This supplementary income can grow over time into a significant contributor to your overall earnings. Additionally, investing in assets such as stocks, bonds, real estate, or even starting a small business can provide additional streams of revenue. These investments require careful consideration and possibly some initial capital, but they offer the potential for passive income streams that grow over time.

Moreover, leveraging digital platforms and technology can expand your reach and income potential. For instance, creating an online store, offering digital products or services, or participating in the gig economy through platforms like freelancing websites or rideshare apps can diversify your income streams without requiring substantial upfront investment. These opportunities allow you to tap into a global market and generate income beyond traditional geographical boundaries.

Furthermore, cultivating multiple income streams encourages creativity and innovation. It encourages individuals to explore new skills, passions, or business ideas that may not have been feasible with a single income source. This diversification not only increases financial security but also fosters a mindset of entrepreneurship and resilience, crucial qualities in today's dynamic economy. By continuously evaluating and optimizing your various income streams, you can create a robust financial foundation that supports your goals and aspirations over the long term.

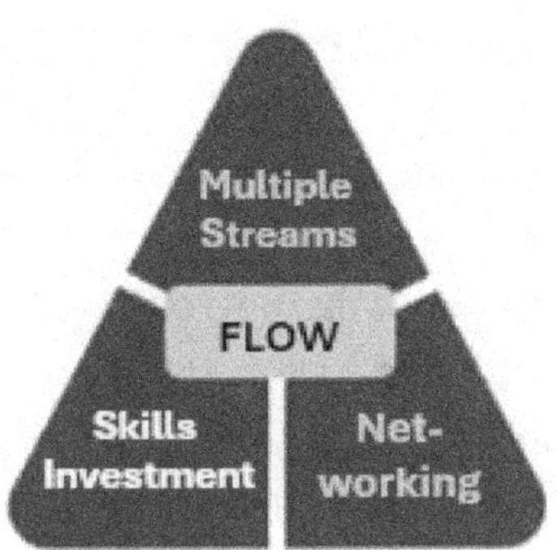
Multiple
Streams
FLOW
Skills
Investment
Net-
working

Skills Investment

Investing in job skills is paramount to making yourself indispensable and highly valuable in today's competitive business landscape. Continuously honing and expanding your skills not only enhances your ability to perform effectively in your current role but also prepares you for future opportunities and challenges. In a rapidly evolving economy driven by technological advancements and changing market demands, staying stagnant in skill development can quickly render you obsolete. Therefore, taking proactive steps to upgrade your skill set ensures that you remain adaptable and capable of adding significant value to any organization.

Moreover, investing in job skills demonstrates a commitment to professional growth and improvement, traits that employers highly value. Whether through formal education, certifications, workshops, or self-paced learning online, acquiring new skills signals to employers that you are proactive, motivated, and dedicated to advancing your career. This proactive approach not only enhances your job performance but also positions you as a valuable asset who can contribute to the organization's success and innovation.

Furthermore, staying abreast of industry trends and acquiring specialized skills can differentiate you from your peers and open doors to new opportunities. Employers increasingly seek candidates who possess not only technical proficiency but also the ability to adapt to changing business environments and contribute to strategic initiatives. By investing in job skills that align with emerging technologies or industry demands, you position yourself as a forward-thinking professional capable of driving growth and innovation within your organization. Ultimately, continuous investment in job skills not only enhances your employability but also empowers you to shape your career trajectory and achieve long-term success in the dynamic world of business.

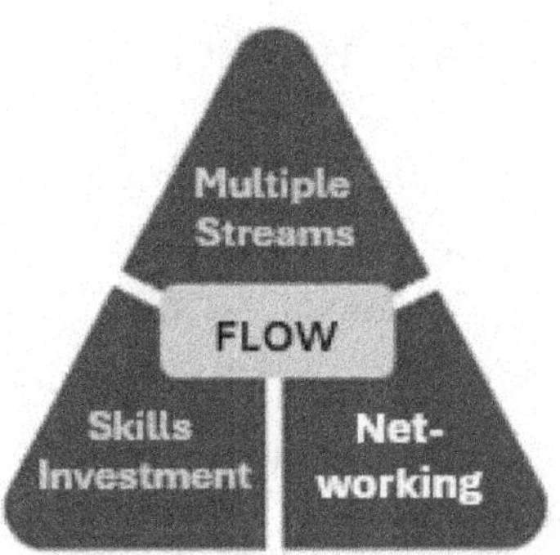
Multiple
Streams
FLOW
Skills
Investment
Net-
working

Networking

Networking on a regular basis is a strategic investment in your professional growth and financial gain. Building and maintaining a strong network of professional contacts opens doors to new opportunities, whether it's securing a higher-paying job, landing lucrative contracts, or gaining valuable insights into industry trends and market developments. Networking allows you to tap into a pool of resources, expertise, and connections that can significantly enhance your career trajectory and financial prospects.

One key benefit of networking is its ability to foster relationships that lead to referrals and recommendations. Many job opportunities and business deals are found through referrals rather than traditional job postings or cold applications. By nurturing relationships with peers, mentors, industry leaders, and potential clients, you increase your visibility and credibility within your professional community. This can translate into more referrals, which often result in higher-quality opportunities that are not publicly advertised.

Furthermore, networking provides access to insider knowledge and information that can give you a competitive edge in your field. Engaging in industry events, conferences, seminars, and online communities allows you to stay informed about market trends, upcoming projects, and potential collaborations. This knowledge empowers you to make informed decisions about career moves, investments, or business ventures, thereby maximizing your financial gain and minimizing risks.

Additionally, networking cultivates a supportive community of like-minded professionals who can offer advice, mentorship, and moral support throughout your career journey. These relationships can provide valuable guidance during times of uncertainty or career transitions, helping you navigate challenges and seize opportunities for growth. By actively participating in networking activities and maintaining genuine connections, you not only enhance your financial gain but also build a strong foundation for long-term career success and personal fulfillment.

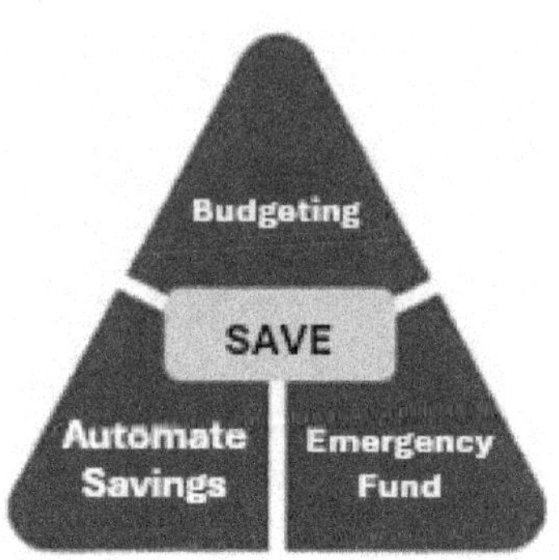
Budgeting
SAVE
Automate
Savings
Emergency
Fund

SAVE

Paying yourself first isn't just about finances—it's a philosophy that can transform how you approach your goals and wellbeing. Imagine your paycheck as a fresh batch of cookies straight out of the oven. Before you start handing them out to everyone else (bills, groceries, that cute new outfit you spotted), you take a moment to set aside a few for yourself. It's not selfish; it's smart. By putting aside, a portion of your income right off the bat—whether it's for savings, investments, or your rainy-day fund—you're ensuring that your future needs are covered.

Think of it like tending to your own garden before watering your neighbor's plants. When you prioritize yourself financially, you're setting the stage for greater peace of mind and security down the road. It's like giving a little gift to your future self—a gesture that says, "I've got your back." Whether you're squirreling away for that dream vacation, building an emergency fund, or investing in your long-term goals, paying yourself first is a powerful habit that builds financial resilience and confidence.

Moreover, paying yourself first isn't just about money; it's a mindset that can spill over into other areas of your life. It teaches you the value of self-care and the importance of nurturing your own dreams alongside your responsibilities. By making this a habit, you're cultivating a sense of empowerment and control over your financial destiny. It's about taking charge and saying, "I deserve to build a better future for myself." So, next time you're divvying up that paycheck, remember to set aside a slice for you—it's not just about what you're saving, but what you're investing in: your own happiness and peace of mind.

Saving money is a cornerstone of financial security and stability, crucial for protecting your future against unexpected expenses, economic downturns, and retirement planning. Here are three keys to effectively saving money:

1. **Establishing a Budget and Setting Goals**: Creating a budget

is the first step in understanding your income and expenses. It helps identify areas where you can cut back or prioritize savings. Start by tracking your monthly expenses and categorizing them into essentials (like housing, utilities, and groceries) and discretionary spending (like dining out and entertainment). Allocate a portion of your income to savings as a non-negotiable expense, treating it with the same priority as bills or rent. Setting specific savings goals, such as building an emergency fund or saving for a down payment, provides motivation and direction in your financial planning.

2. **Automating Savings and Practicing Frugality**: Automating your savings can make it easier to consistently set aside money without the temptation to spend it. Set up automatic transfers from your checking account to a savings account or retirement fund each payday. This approach ensures that saving becomes a habit rather than an afterthought. Additionally, practicing frugality by consciously reducing unnecessary expenses can free up more funds for savings. This might involve comparison shopping, using coupons or cashback apps, meal planning to reduce food costs, or finding free or low-cost alternatives to expensive activities.

3. **Building an Emergency Fund and Investing Wisely**: An emergency fund acts as a financial buffer against unexpected expenses such as medical bills, car repairs, or job loss. Aim to save enough to cover three to six months' worth of living expenses. Keep this fund in a liquid account (like a savings account) that allows easy access in times of need. Once your emergency fund is established, consider investing for long-term financial growth. This may include contributing to retirement accounts (like 401(k)s or IRAs), diversified investment portfolios, or real estate. Understanding your risk tolerance and seeking professional advice can help you make informed

decisions that align with your financial goals and timeline.

By implementing these keys—establishing a budget and goals, automating savings, practicing frugality, building an emergency fund, and investing wisely—you can safeguard your financial future and create a solid foundation for achieving your long-term financial aspirations.

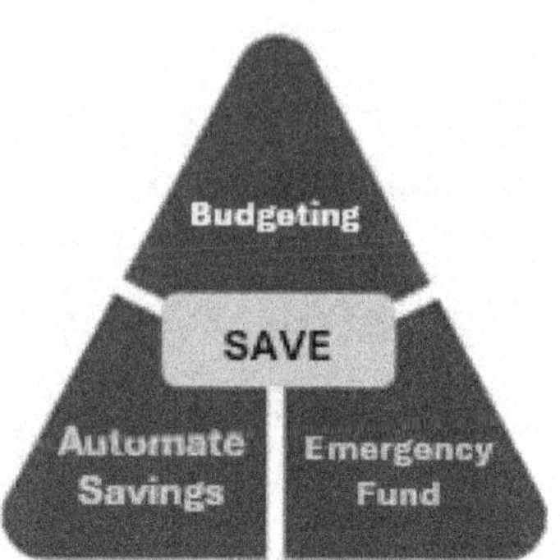
Budgeting
SAVE
Automate
Savings
Emergency
Fund

Budgeting

Budgeting on a regular basis is essential for safeguarding your financial interests and ensuring long-term financial stability. A budget serves as a roadmap that helps you track income, manage expenses, and allocate funds strategically. By establishing a budget, you gain a clear understanding of where your money is going each month, which allows you to make informed decisions about spending and saving. This awareness is crucial in identifying unnecessary expenditures, reducing debt, and prioritizing financial goals such as building savings or investing for the future.

Moreover, budgeting empowers you to live within your means and avoid overspending. It promotes responsible financial behavior by setting limits on discretionary spending and encouraging thoughtful consumption. By adhering to a budget, you can avoid accumulating debt and maintain a healthy financial outlook. This discipline not only protects your current financial interests but also prepares you for unexpected expenses or economic uncertainties that may arise.

Additionally, regular budgeting cultivates financial discipline and accountability. It encourages proactive financial planning and enables you to adjust your spending habits as needed to align with your financial goals. Whether you're saving for a major purchase, planning for retirement, or managing day-to-day expenses, a well-maintained budget provides the framework for making informed financial decisions and achieving long-term financial success. Ultimately, budgeting on a regular basis fosters financial mindfulness, empowers you to take control of your financial future, and ensures that your financial interests are protected over time.

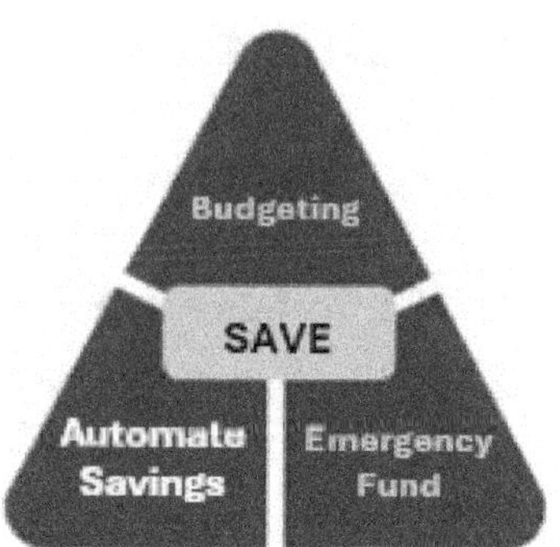
Budgeting
SAVE
Automate Savings
Emergency Fund

Automate Savings

Automating your savings is a powerful strategy for achieving financial stability and building wealth over time. By setting up automatic transfers from your checking account to a designated savings or investment account, you ensure that saving becomes a consistent and non-negotiable part of your financial routine. This approach eliminates the temptation to spend money that you intended to save, as the process occurs seamlessly in the background. Automating savings instills discipline and helps you prioritize long-term financial goals, such as building an emergency fund, saving for a down payment on a home, or funding your retirement.

In addition, automating savings cultivates financial consistency and reduces the likelihood of missing savings targets. Rather than relying on sporadic manual deposits, automation ensures that funds are consistently set aside according to your predetermined savings plan. This reliability is crucial for achieving financial stability and weathering economic fluctuations or unexpected expenses without compromising your financial goals. Automating savings also encourages financial mindfulness by establishing a habit of regular saving, regardless of fluctuations in income or expenses.

Finally, automating savings can help you take advantage of compound interest and investment growth over time. By consistently contributing to savings or investment accounts, you allow your money to grow exponentially through interest or returns on investments. This passive growth can significantly enhance your financial stability and security in the long run, providing a cushion against inflation and helping you achieve greater financial independence. Ultimately, automating your savings streamlines your financial management, reinforces disciplined saving habits, and accelerates progress towards achieving your financial objectives.

Budgeting
SAVE
Automate
Savings
Emergency
Fund

Emergency Fund

Having a financial emergency fund is crucial for safeguarding your money situation and providing a buffer against unexpected expenses or financial setbacks. An emergency fund serves as a financial safety net, allowing you to cover urgent expenses without resorting to high-interest debt or depleting your savings earmarked for other goals. Whether it's a medical emergency, car repairs, sudden job loss, or home repairs, having readily accessible funds in an emergency fund ensures that you can navigate these challenges with minimal financial stress.

Moreover, an emergency fund provides peace of mind and financial security. Knowing that you have funds set aside specifically for unforeseen circumstances allows you to face uncertainties with confidence and resilience. This peace of mind extends beyond immediate financial needs; it also enables you to focus on long-term financial goals, such as saving for retirement, investing in education, or purchasing a home, without the constant worry of unexpected expenses derailing your plans.

Additionally, an emergency fund promotes financial independence and stability. It reduces reliance on credit cards or loans during emergencies, which can lead to debt accumulation and financial strain over time. By proactively building and maintaining an emergency fund, you take control of your financial future and strengthen your overall financial health. Ideally, aim to save enough in your emergency fund to cover three to six months' worth of living expenses. This cushion provides a buffer against temporary income disruptions and allows you to maintain your standard of living until you can secure alternative income sources.

In conclusion, having a financial emergency fund is not just a prudent financial strategy; it is a cornerstone of financial preparedness and resilience. It empowers you to weather financial storms, navigate unexpected challenges, and pursue your long-term financial goals with confidence. By prioritizing the establishment and maintenance of an emergency fund, you safeguard your money situation and build a solid foundation for achieving financial stability and independence over the long term.

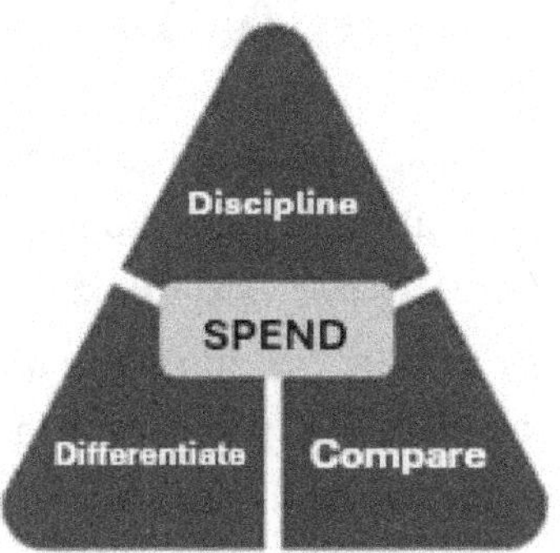
Discipline
SPEND
Differentiate
Compare

SPEND

Spending wisely is like navigating through a buffet—there are so many tempting options, but you know that loading up on everything might not leave you feeling your best afterward. It's about making choices that align with your priorities and long-term goals. When you spend wisely, you're not just stretching your dollars; you're investing in what truly matters to you. Whether it's saving up for that dream vacation, building a nest egg, or supporting causes close to your heart, every dollar spent thoughtfully is a step toward financial freedom and peace of mind.

Think of it as building a sturdy house—one where each brick is carefully chosen to withstand the test of time. When you make intentional spending decisions, you're laying a foundation for a more secure future. It's not about depriving yourself of joy but finding ways to maximize the value you get from every dollar. Whether you're comparing prices, hunting for deals, or simply pausing to ask yourself, "Do I really need this?" you're cultivating a habit that pays off in more ways than one.

Moreover, spending wisely isn't just about the numbers; it's about fostering a mindset of gratitude and contentment. It's recognizing the difference between fleeting impulses and lasting satisfaction. By making conscious choices about where your money goes, you're not only shaping your financial landscape but also cultivating a sense of empowerment and control over your life. So, next time you reach for your wallet, remember that each purchase is an opportunity to invest in your future—choose wisely, and watch your dreams take shape.

Spending wisely is essential for managing finances effectively and achieving money stability. Here are three keys to help you spend wisely:

1. **Create and Stick to a Budget**: Establishing a budget is fundamental to wise spending. Start by tracking your income and categorizing your expenses into essentials (such as housing, utilities, groceries) and discretionary items (like dining out,

entertainment). Allocate specific amounts for each category based on your income and financial goals. Regularly review your budget to ensure you're staying within your limits and adjust as necessary to accommodate changing circumstances. By adhering to a budget, you prioritize essential expenses while curbing unnecessary spending, which is crucial for maintaining financial stability.

2. **Differentiate Between Needs and Wants**: Practicing discernment between needs and wants is key to spending wisely. Needs are essential for survival and maintaining a basic standard of living, while wants are non-essential desires or luxuries. Before making a purchase, evaluate whether it fulfills a genuine need or if it's a discretionary expense that can be postponed or eliminated. This mindset shift helps you prioritize spending on necessities while minimizing impulse purchases or frivolous expenditures that can strain your finances. Consider implementing a waiting period for non-essential purchases to avoid impulse buying and ensure that your spending aligns with your financial priorities and goals.

3. **Comparison Shopping and Practicing Frugality**: Comparison shopping allows you to find the best value for your money on essential purchases, from groceries to big-ticket items like electronics or furniture. Researching prices, reading reviews, and exploring discounts or promotions can help you save significantly over time. Additionally, practicing frugality involves finding ways to reduce costs without sacrificing quality of life. This could include using coupons, buying items second-hand, negotiating better deals, or opting for cost-effective alternatives. By adopting these habits, you stretch your dollars further and optimize your spending, contributing to long-term financial stability and security.

By implementing these keys—creating and sticking to a budget, differentiating between needs and wants, and practicing comparison shopping and frugality—you can cultivate smart spending habits that support financial stability and contribute to achieving your financial goals over time.

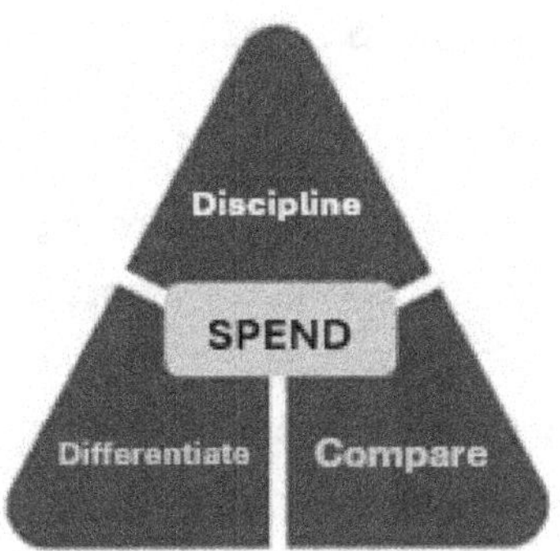
Discipline
SPEND
Differentiate
Compare

Discipline

Discipline in managing money is crucial for achieving financial goals, maintaining stability, and securing long-term financial well-being. Financial discipline involves making deliberate and informed decisions about spending, saving, and investing, guided by a commitment to fiscal responsibility and prudent financial management. It requires self-control, consistency, and a strategic approach to budgeting, saving, and prioritizing financial objectives.

One of the key benefits of financial discipline is the ability to resist impulse purchases and unnecessary expenditures. By adhering to a budget and distinguishing between needs and wants, individuals can avoid falling into the trap of overspending or accumulating debt. This disciplined approach not only preserves financial resources but also cultivates a mindset of mindful consumption, where every financial decision contributes to broader financial objectives and stability.

Financial discipline enables individuals to build and maintain emergency savings and retirement funds. By consistently setting aside a portion of income for savings and investments, disciplined savers create a financial cushion that protects against unforeseen expenses and economic downturns. This proactive planning fosters resilience and reduces reliance on credit or loans during financial emergencies, safeguarding financial security and peace of mind.

Finally, financial discipline extends beyond day-to-day budgeting; it encompasses long-term financial planning and goal setting. Whether saving for a home, funding education, or preparing for retirement, disciplined financial habits ensure that individuals stay on track to achieve their aspirations. This involves setting clear financial goals, establishing timelines, and regularly evaluating progress. By maintaining discipline and staying focused on financial objectives, individuals can build wealth, achieve financial independence, and enjoy greater financial freedom and opportunities in the future.

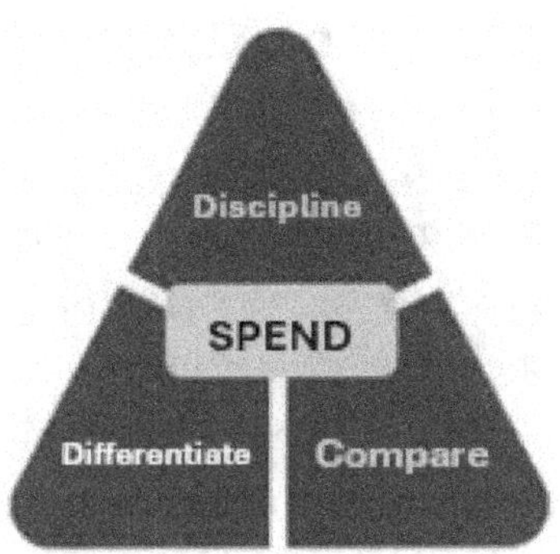
Discipline
SPEND
Differentiate
Compare

Differentiate

Understanding the distinction between needs and wants is fundamental to making sound financial decisions and achieving financial stability. **Needs** are essential goods and services necessary for basic living and survival, such as food, shelter, clothing, healthcare, and transportation. These expenditures are non-negotiable and typically take priority in budgeting and financial planning. On the other hand, **wants** are desires or luxuries that enhance quality of life but are not essential for survival, such as dining out, entertainment, travel, and luxury items. Recognizing and prioritizing needs versus wants allows individuals to allocate resources efficiently and responsibly, ensuring that essential expenses are met before discretionary spending.

Practicing discernment between needs and wants is crucial for maintaining financial health and avoiding overspending or accumulating debt. By prioritizing needs and limiting discretionary expenses, individuals can live within their means and build a solid financial foundation. This disciplined approach not only ensures financial stability in the short term but also supports long-term financial goals such as saving for emergencies, retirement, or major purchases. Moreover, differentiating between needs and wants encourages mindful consumption and cultivates a habit of responsible financial behavior.

Understanding the difference between needs and wants empowers individuals to make intentional spending decisions that align with their values and financial priorities. It encourages thoughtful evaluation of purchases based on their utility, value, and impact on overall financial well-being. By focusing resources on fulfilling genuine needs and selectively indulging in wants that align with personal goals and values, individuals can achieve a balanced and fulfilling financial life. Ultimately, mastering the art of distinguishing between needs and wants promotes financial mindfulness, enhances financial security, and empowers individuals to achieve greater financial freedom and success over time.

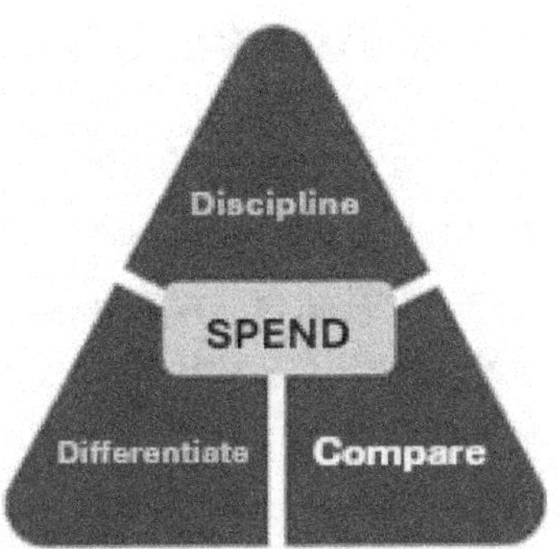
Discipline
SPEND
Differentiate
Compare

Compare

Comparison shopping plays a crucial role in enhancing one's financial status by allowing individuals to make informed purchasing decisions that maximize value and minimize unnecessary expenses. Whether you're buying groceries, electronics, insurance policies, or even services like home repairs, comparing prices and features enables you to identify the best deals and save money over time. This practice empowers consumers to leverage their purchasing power effectively, ensuring that every dollar spent delivers maximum benefit.

Also, comparison shopping encourages competition among retailers and service providers, which often leads to lower prices and improved offerings for consumers. By actively seeking out the best deals and promotions, you not only save money on immediate purchases but also create a habit of financial mindfulness and efficiency. This approach is particularly valuable in today's digital age, where online platforms and mobile apps make it easier than ever to compare prices, read reviews, and access customer feedback before making a purchase decision.

Finally, comparison shopping extends beyond just finding the lowest price; it involves evaluating quality, reliability, and customer satisfaction. By researching products or services before buying, you can ensure that you're getting the best value for your money without compromising on quality. This prudent approach not only enhances your financial status by reducing unnecessary spending but also contributes to long-term financial health and stability. Ultimately, comparison shopping empowers individuals to make informed choices, optimize their spending, and achieve greater financial security and success in both the short and long term.

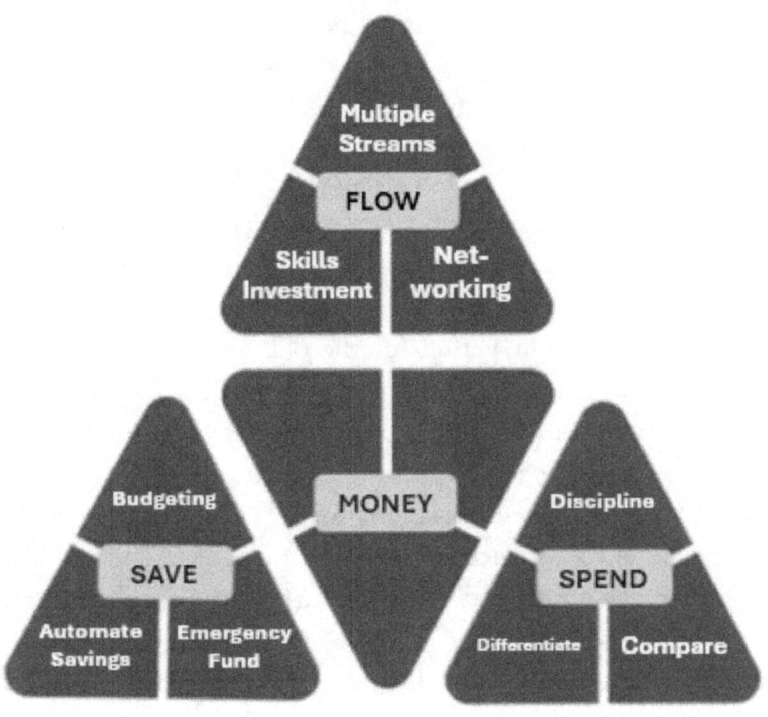
Multiple
Streams
FLOW
Skills
Investment
Net-
working
Budgeting
MONEY
Discipline
SAVE
SPEND
Automate
Savings
Emergency
Fund
Differentiate
Compare

SUMMARY

The transition from old currency to new currency is a complex process that involves economic, logistical, and societal considerations. Countries may decide to introduce new currency for various reasons, such as combating counterfeiting, updating security features, addressing inflationary pressures, or aligning with international standards. This transition typically begins with the announcement of the new currency, followed by a phase-out period for the old currency to be gradually withdrawn from circulation. During this transition, governments and central banks work closely with financial institutions and businesses to ensure a smooth exchange process for the public.

One of the primary motivations for replacing old currency with new currency is to enhance security and reduce counterfeiting risks. Modern currency designs often incorporate advanced security features such as holograms, watermarks, and color-shifting inks that make it more difficult to counterfeit. By introducing new currency, authorities aim to bolster confidence in the monetary system and protect the integrity of the national currency.

Moreover, the introduction of new currency may also be driven by technological advancements and the need to modernize payment systems. New currency designs may include features that facilitate electronic transactions, improve durability, or integrate with digital payment platforms. This evolution reflects broader trends towards a cashless society and the increasing adoption of digital and mobile payment solutions.

In conclusion, while the transition from old currency to new currency involves logistical challenges and requires careful planning, it represents an opportunity for countries to enhance security, improve functionality, and adapt to evolving economic and technological landscapes. By effectively managing this transition, governments can strengthen monetary stability, foster public trust in the financial system, and position their economies for future growth and innovation.

Invitation

A credit score is a critical measure of financial responsibility and reliability for both individuals and businesses, influencing access to credit, loan terms, and even opportunities for growth. For individuals, maintaining a good credit score is essential for accessing favorable interest rates on mortgages, auto loans, and credit cards. A high credit score indicates to lenders that an individual is likely to repay debts responsibly, which can result in lower borrowing costs and better financial terms over time. It also expands access to credit options during emergencies or when making significant purchases, providing flexibility in managing personal finances.

Similarly, businesses rely on credit scores to establish credibility with suppliers, investors, and lenders. A strong business credit score enhances access to capital for expansion, operational needs, or investment in new ventures. It also facilitates favorable terms on loans and trade credit, enabling businesses to manage cash flow effectively and seize growth opportunities. A positive credit history can open doors to partnerships, contracts, and favorable vendor relationships, as it demonstrates reliability and financial stability to stakeholders.

Maintaining a good credit score requires responsible financial management, including making timely payments on debts, managing credit utilization effectively, and minimizing outstanding balances. Regularly monitoring credit reports allows individuals and businesses to identify and address inaccuracies or issues that could impact their creditworthiness. By prioritizing good credit practices, individuals and businesses can strengthen their financial status, improve access to financial resources, and position themselves for long-term success in both personal and business endeavors.

I have found that working with a credit service helps stay on top of issues such as identity theft, bad reporting by credit companies and old issues that need to be removed.

When you're with someone who is sharing their struggles with you...just smile at him/her and give them one of these. He/she will ask "What is that?" Then simply reply "Life Works in Threes."

Quotes about Money

1. "Money is only a tool. It will take you wherever you wish, but it will not replace you as the driver." – Ayn Rand

1. "A wise person should have money in their head, but not in their heart." – Jonathan Swift

1. "Money often costs too much."   Ralph Waldo Emerson

1. "It's not your salary that makes you rich, it's your spending habits." – Charles A. Jaffe

1. "The art is not in making money, but in keeping it." – Proverb

1. "Money is a terrible master but an excellent servant." – P.T. Barnum

1. "Money is usually attracted, not pursued." – Jim Rohn

1. "Time is more valuable than money. You can get more money, but you cannot get more time." – Jim Rohn

1. "The lack of money is the root of all evil." – Mark Twain

1. "Money can't buy happiness, but it can make you awfully comfortable while you're being miserable." – Clare Boothe Luce

Other titles coming out:

- Weight Struggles?
- Abundance Struggles?
- Parenting Struggles?
- Life Struggles?
- Purpose Struggles?
- Happiness Struggles?
- Sales Struggles?
- Speaker Struggles?
- Time Struggles?
- Network Struggles?
- Marriage Struggles?
- Divorce Struggles?
- Romance Struggles?
- Career Struggles?
- Dating Struggles?
- Caretaker Struggles?
- Forgiveness Struggles?
- Grieving Struggles?
- Success Struggles?
- Golf Struggles?
- Workplace Struggles?
- Stress Struggles?
- Shame/Guilt Struggles?
- Addiction Struggles?

Remember,
When you get right down to it,
Life is about making choices.

Every day, all day long, that's what we do.

- *We choose to get out of bed or not.*
- *We choose to clean up or not.*
- *We choose what to eat all day.*
- *We choose to exercise or not.*
- *We choose to go to work or not.*
- *We choose to do a good job or not.*
- *We choose to come home or not.*
- *We choose to watch TV or do something constructive.*
- *We choose to bed at a decent hour or not.*

And the next day...we start all over again.
What is the meaning of this? Get good at choosing.
Before you can get good at choosing though...you need to understand how life works in threes.

When someone is struggling with a particular area or two, chances are they are "out of balance" with how life works. How does life work? Life works in threes.

If you're interested in personal topics like life, health, money or business topics like sales, time management and public speaking...Life Works In Threes! can shed some light on creating success in those areas.

The definition of TRIUNE is a group of three things; united. Being three in one, such as - humans are *mental, physical* and *spiritual beings.* The word TRYUNE is a play of the word TRIUNE, encouraging all to try this concept and help eliminate struggling unnecessarily.

LifeWorksInThrees.com